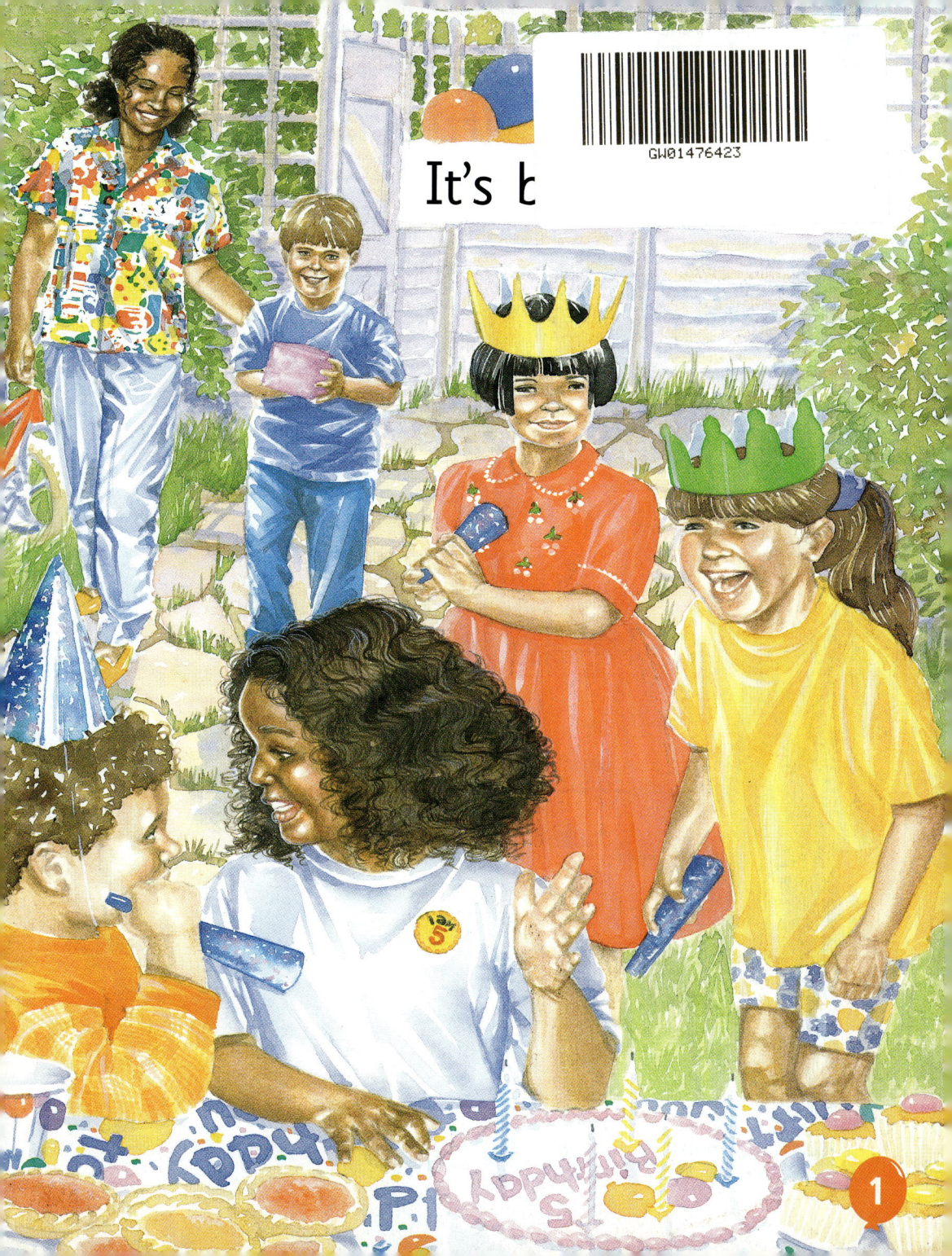

When I was little,
I could not ride my bike.

I had to get Mum or Dad to help me.

I can ride it very fast.

When I was little,
I could not read my books.

I had to get Mum or Dad to read them to me.

But now I am five,
I can read my books.

I can read books like this one.

When I was little,
I could not get some water.

I had to get Mum or Dad to do it for me.

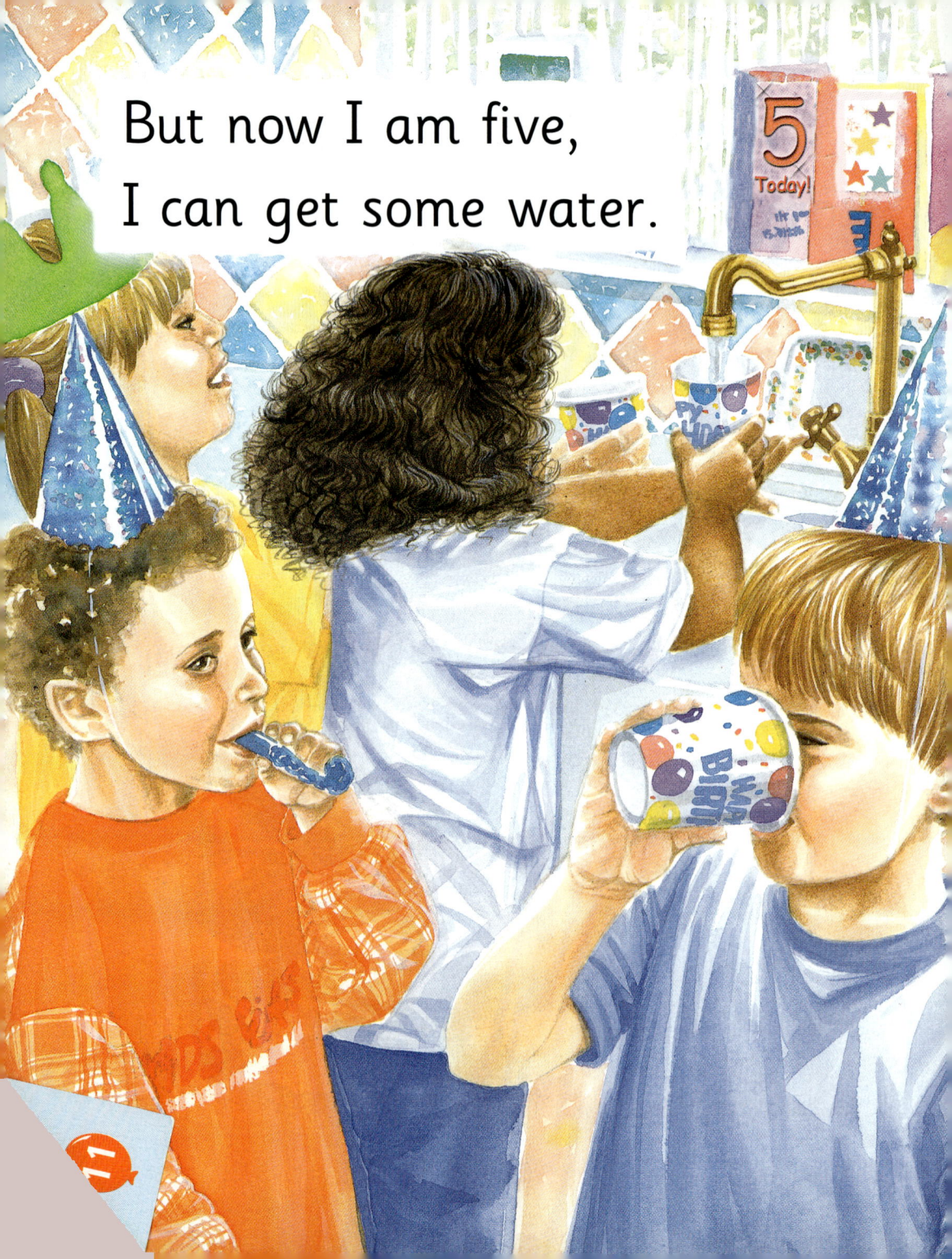
But now I am five,
I can get some water.

When I was little,
I had a teddy.

You can still have a teddy when you are five.

It's best to be five!

Index

bike **2, 4**
books **6, 8, 9**

Dad **3, 7, 11**

Mum **3, 7, 11**

teddy **13, 14**

water **10, 12**